Within the Light

Helene Castles

Within the Light

I appreciate the support given to me by my family,
and my friends, past and present, from the
Goulburn Valley Writers' Group.
Thank you to Pat Patt for the final edit before sending
the manuscript to Ginninderra Press for publication.

For Charlie

Within the Light
ISBN 978 1 76109 142 1
Copyright © text Helene Castles 2021
Cover design: Creagh Manning
Cover image: Helix Nebula, courtesy of NASA's Hubble Telescope

First published 2021 by
GINNINDERRA PRESS
PO Box 3461 Port Adelaide 5015
www.ginninderrapress.com.au

Contents

Preface	9
Appraisal	11
Theology Overload	12
Soul of the Earth	13
Artisan's Reveal	14
Hibernation	15
Winton	16
Melbourne Street Talk	17
Speaking of Language	19
Superb Fairy Wren	20
Pelican	21
The Nook	22
Manipulation	24
Temple of the Universe	25
Gridlocks & Gophers	26
Tumble Down at Toombullup	29
Pink Posy	30
Negotiation	31
Boarding School in the Fifties	32
Southern Ocean Live Show	33
Where the Poems Hide	34
Seeds of Summer	35
Coffee Time	36
Lake Tekapo	37
Queenstown Camping	38
Puddle-talk	39
The Mulberry Tree	40
A Case of Google-itis	41
Woomera – Refugees' Day Out At the Animal Park	43
Palm Beach	44

St Paul's Cathedral	45
Rhythm of the Night	47
The Promise	48
Layers of a Storm	49
The Cusp of Love	50
Within the Light	51
Goats You Said	52
Liberty	53
Observation	54
This Time of Life	55
Cyclical Changes	56
Dancing Brolgas	57
Colours of a Winter's Night	58
Bush Meditation	59
Expression – At Site Sixteen	60
'Banksia' Poetry Group – 2019	62
Migration	63
Winter in the Washhouse	64
Alaphilippe	66
Kaleidoscope	67
Newell Highway – 2019	68
Drought	69
Art in the Singing Garden	70
Big Dam	71
Death of a Star – Hen 2-437	72
Hailstorm	73
Wax Print Fabric Bag – Design No. 13455	74
When the Bubble Bursts	76
Pins, Poems and Protocol	77
Horoscope	78
Norfolk Island	79
Full Moon at Winton Wetlands	80

Blue Moon 2018	81
Leaving the City	82
Maypole	83
Spare	84
Gratitude	86
Ode to Quasimodo	87
Cinquain	90
Australian Identity	91
Cosmic Dig	92
Remember	93
Festival Art	94
Mysterious Bird	95
Breakdown	96
#Beachwalk@80	97
Storm	98
A Chance Meeting	99
Union of the Arts	100
Pressed Flower	102
No Through Road	103
Windsong	104
Buddhist Sound Bath	105
The Colour of Love	106
When Summer Burns	107
Self-isolation	108
The Poet's Climate Prophecy	109
A Moment in Time	111
Supermarket Dilemma	112
The Final Edit	113
Acknowledgements	114

Preface

There is no perfect, logical scheme. The poems in this collection have been given free play as individuals. Some are linked by subject, time, or place.

You might pick up a poetry book occasionally, to read one or two poems, or read cover to cover and follow the sensory seam that automatically flows through any collection of poems by one author.

As we live, we learn that history repeats itself. There will always be another way to say it.

Poems need readers to nourish them and give them life.

The enterprise is completed with the sharing.

Helene Castles

Appraisal

The wind soughs smooth round the boundaries
softens the ground at my feet
reminds me I cannot return
to the random beliefs of my time.

A vortex whirls keen round my habits
the tide and the currents rush by
I cannot let go of the pace
the wind soughs smooth round the boundaries.

I listen and pitch all the sounds
to the teachings I keep with me now
the sense of the peace in this sanctuary
softens the ground at my feet.

The pine trees distorted with age
whisper appraisals to me
my people now perished by time
remind me I cannot return.

Tossing the far-flung remorse
to cessation in form of a trance
I apportion the trance   deal a hand
to the random beliefs of my time.

Futility flounces her skirts
embroiders the future with plans
to texture the way that I'm living,
an end to an end – and I'm hearing
the wind sough smooth.

Theology Overload

On a Sunday morning at St Peter's Eastern Hill,
Father Maynard's sermon put *himself* to sleep.

His speech wavered, then he nodded off,
chin clamping down onto his chest.

Shocked, he woke seconds later;
preached the homily from where he'd stopped.

With chapel service daily at five o'clock,
church, morning and evening on Sundays,

my brain covertly soaked up the ancient texts,
the psalms, hymns and gospels, and stowed them.

Unprepared for the complexities of adulthood,
the subconscious worked through layers of doctrine,

appreciated the cadence, whittled down the material:
with a myriad store of quotes and a head full of notes,

cleared the debris, treasured the poetry; found clarity
and cause in the essentials of Christianity.

Soul of the Earth

The knowledge of man is as the waters, some descending from above, and some springing from beneath… – Francis Bacon

Devoid of the notion of the ways of the world,
away from the light of nature down there;
still water in the house well, cold and clean.

Filling and refilling, fresh from the springhead,
oblivious to the perils of the life will;
devoid of the notion of the ways of the world.

Rains descend, filling cracks and crevices,
speculative, probing depths of thirsting soil;
still water in the house well, cold and clean.

Water weeping down, wetting tree roots,
seeping into the soul of the earth, a whispered prayer;
devoid of the notion of the ways of the world.

Subtle the intrusion, replenishing underground streams,
soaking, operative there in the dark earth;
still water in the house well, cold and clean.

Hand pump, lift-push – drawing first splash of water,
lift-push – gushing, unhindered, into the tin utensil,
devoid of the notion of the ways of the world,
still water in the house well, cold and clean.

Artisan's Reveal

Coals shimmer white hot.
Strong arms pump the bellows
hands roll the tempered iron
over and over in the forge.

Hammer on anvil
plies the glowing rod.
BANG   BANG   BANG
flipping   shaping
BANG
heating   turning
BANG   BANG   BANG

Sizzle of the cooling head
hissing in the water pail
hands dip the steaming rod
in and out
twirling
holding to the light.

Hibernation

This black is the black of the cave base,
    the light that streams in at the cave face
    casts shadows that hang on the rock walls.
Black from the black of the cave base,
cuts off the span of the light beam,
    dark energy spreading a pall
    over the whispering *thrm thrm* of the bats,
to shadows that hang on the rock walls:
the sudden shudder of comfort, to stillness.
    The aura that held the essence of life,
    diffused in the darkness, departs with the light,
dormant, a life form, heedless they sleep.

Winton

for Kathleen

bucket and knife
picking mushrooms…
step inside a fairy ring

                limpid water
                ice lids on puddles...
                school inspector's car

hollow thud at dawn
hobnail boots on lino…
a dog chain rattles

                sheep in a mob
                two stragglers…
                go way back

unwelcome intruder
writhing brown snake…
a bull ants' hill

                lake bed cracked mud
                concrete chunks scattered…
                rattle of roller skates

Melbourne Street Talk

The new goodbye is love-you!
For all the people, him or her,
you hear them talking home and work,
flippant as a warm weekend
or anxious in the busy street –
there's rhythm in the city's words.

A tall man speaks, alone with words
he's twirling cords, he looks at you,
keeps his line in Swanston Street,
concentrates he chats to her,
until the theme of their weekend
he gifts you as he walks to work.

Some vocalise their lives at work.
You pause and watch, tuned in to words
about the Cup and last weekend,
as if it should be known to you –
and tangled in the talk to her,
is talk to you. You cross the street,

the lights are green; this is the street
you know so well. They're leaving work,
the mobile phones with him with her,
drench the street with love-you words –
and bonhomie returns to you!
A woman speaks of this weekend,

you contemplate your own weekend,
as Friday chatter fills the street.
Easing through the swarming crowd,
you walk the final block to work,
wend your way through city's words.
The woman smiles, you smile at her,

not knowing what's ahead for her.
Who could know this sad week's end?
The biosphere is teeming words,
there's fear and evil in your street.
You know you must return to work –
there Melbourne cast her spell on you.

A smile for her, now work must wait,
as on the frenzied fiery street,
he watches; he is heeding you
approaching him, with kindly words:
'Now wait! Wait please!'
His knife is drawn: *Ciao! Love you!*

In 2018 Sisto Malaspina, co-owner of Pellegrini's Coffee Bar, was killed in a terrorist attack in Bourke Street, Melbourne.

Speaking of Language

Throbs of fading silence
searching for the words

listen for the language
see how it sings

Barramundi   Dingo
song drenched spirits

Jabiru and Billabong
and dragonfly wings.

Dhuwa   Yirridtja
lyrics of your song

painted songs of passion
Charcoal   Yellow Clay

mystery in the meaning
motivating senses

communal waters streaming
   a Live Show:
       'the way'.

Dhuwa   Yirridtja from *Story About Feeling*, Bill Neidjie
3rd prize Ruqayyah Ibourki Ekphrasis Poetry Competition, 2018

Superb Fairy Wren

Winton Wetlands

Perches
tail flicking
light and airy
flutters onto clusters of straw
worries stem to stem
avian fairy
frets
poses momentarily
flick-flits away.

Pelican

Idled –
high on the brown water
wings limp
large beak
dipped to drink,
head back to swallow
drifted
watched us –
lifted
webbed feet down
skimmed the channel
once   twice   three times:
flew lumbered away.

The Nook

1950, Tarnook, north-east Victoria

At first glance the paddocks looked like any common piece
of unproductive land.
A mass of hungry rabbits grazed the gravelled slopes;
a grey, mute, marauding band.

Red and orange rock, no roots to hold the earth.
Rabbits moved through, fence to fence,
and the winds blew, harvesting loose soil, stealing
with decisive sleight-of-hand.

Deep gullies formed in swaths across the paddocks,
pasture eroded, soil loosened.
Birds burrowed nests in broken-earth walls. In and out
they flew, in the ever-changing land.

Gums cast their sentry shadows along the lane, silence
clicking with the seasons' beat.
A way of life! The dogs, the ute; each day another
monumental task at hand.

Lunch box packed, stock to feed, stumps to burn,
outrage meddling with the mind;
resolve the only posture against the shifting sand.
The Nook was still, in some ways, grand.

Spring grass grew, warrens alive with young,
the cycle of destruction began again.
Surrendering to the stress, the farmers knew
sheer numbers put the rabbits in command.

Advancing on both fronts, tunnel erosion two feet deep,
they travelled underground.
Unrelenting the constant march of this unwitting foe,
this awful contraband.

Above ground, the earth crawled with rabbits; sheep foraging
for burrs and seeds.
Seasons came and seasons passed. Life continued, harshly
controlled by the fractured land.

The morning rounds – in just one day, the lives of farmers
and the stock transformed.
Annihilation! Rabbits dead, some blind, hunched up in pain;
bizarre this final stand.

What had happened? Science could explain. A virus
killed the pests in one cruel sweep.
The vicious strike of myxomatosis had come in the night,
returning a livelihood to the land.

Patiently, with pastoral care, the challenge met head-on,
the Nook was farmed again.
Grasses sown, gullies filled, paddocks restocked:
a doggedness too deep to understand.

Manipulation

Testing backward masking

An outline on the page is making shapes.
The thumb that grips the pen behind the light,
inverts the backward masking, that escapes
and babbles at the shadows of the night.

The cryptic beat manipulates debate,
a sense the tonal message is maligned,
the shadow's interactions then create
a doorway to the shelter of the mind.

An outline at the edges, at the brink
of time and place, the vagaries of phrase,
the soft gel of the pen is spilling ink,
that's flowing, guiding, cursive as it plays

> a game with connotations – overflows;
> fills the page with elevated prose.

Temple of the Universe

In beauty, love, divinity the Deva's powers bide,
to unify the trinity, infuse galactic light,
that spreads an arc, an energy, emerging into sight.
The deity remaps the spirit guide.

Star seed workers congregate to rearrange the code,
explosions borne of synergy, foment a simple test,
to gather and assimilate energies thought best,
foretelling of a safe, but winding road.

The Gaia and the Titans, the bearers of the light;
their mission is to liberate the star-crossed soul of man.
Ancestral mother reads the script and validates the plan,
while basking in the limpid, silver night.

Cosmic shifts and variables; the moon, the stars, the tides –
a number locks the sequence – planets realigned.
Ancient downloads, lineage, considered and defined,
our fortunes told in prophesies by Zodiacal Guides.

Gridlocks & Gophers

Snakes draped, black or brown on garden fence;
we're told they live until the sun goes down.
We trampled down the fleece to fill the bales,
aware the wool press could have been our tomb.

Wheat, the stifling wheat could snuff our lives;
the depth, the silo's freely flowing grain.
Rams, that fought at sundown locking horns,
as lambs pranced on the dam banks, playing games.

A rooster white and proud, with mordant spurs;
we taunted him, tantalised his hens.
He'd fly at us with talons, long and sharp,
he'd dodge the clods, then prance, then go again.

The wrath, the censored wrath of our dear mum.
That shearer can't come back next year! she said.
He washed his greasy clothes in my clean bath!
She scrubbed until the surface lost its sheen.

Waterdogs and *gophers* owned the dam,
dabchicks dipped and dabbed in perfect time;
they lived in peace together. When we swam
they'd gone, the *dogs* and *gophers* – hunting truths.

Tracks into our home that bogged the car,
skidding wheels spun furrows in the mud,
she revved us into silence, then we prayed
for traction, and escape from mother-rage.

A chance that we'd be blown to smithereens,
with gelignite stashed safely in the tree:
the plan was, that the boys might fire a shot!
Informed, we all walked wide, when passing by.

We chose the dam for swimming in the heat,
turned leeches inside-out on skinny sticks.
Yanked from our legs – extreme is our remorse –
they'd sucked our blood, deep in the swill of silt.

Around the house verandas Mum patrolled,
when summer winds fanned sparks from passing trains,
or knapsack on her back, her lonely wrath,
when forced to fight the fires we had lit.

The boys' commotion, gloved up set to spar;
they fought for sport – the sport turned into angst
when blood was spilt. We'd hurry, ring the gong.
Ding-dong, a verdict, then a shake of hands.

The stubble burn, the beauty and the fear,
controlled by chance, the men and Furphy tanks;
flames that lit the evening yellow-red,
paddocks smoking weeds on ashen ground.

At night, a gridlock formed when we arrived.
First in the bath – we argued over turns.
Tea was served with noise, our day was told,
events upheld with question and review,

then father from his bed reciting life
in poetry, the lantern's wick burned low;
the pecking order, flimsy through the day,
enforced in firm extremes in double beds.

Tumble Down at Toombullup

Day blindness – Hemeralopia

You touch the day with sensitive hands,
eyes quiver shut in the glare of the sun.
Full-stretch we roll down the grassy slope.
    The light of your day is a blinding light.

A marvellous feat, enhanced by the risk –
the rush of the river, below the bank.
There's danger, we pause, we're back in control.
    The morning light is a piercing light.

Unsteady we stand as lunch is announced.
We climb the slope in response to the call.
Spent with our efforts, linked by our fears,
    hungry, skipping and laughing, we run.

Steeped in aromas of roasting beef,
pilgrims at Toombullup, ready to feast.
Family and friends gathered for lunch;
    eyes open wide with the chattering noise.

The thin forest trail is soft underfoot,
the canopy shades the afternoon sun.
We bathe in the sounds of chirruping birds,
    the light of your day enhanced by the fun.

When night greets the last of the day, as they pass,
and evening spreads shadows over the world,
the goddess of daylight departs, and you move
    from tension to glow in the gold of the moon.

Pink Posy

Burgundy stems
of belladonna lilies
push through coarse
silver-light gravel
between the monuments.

Swollen veins
burst open overnight
bringing gifts:
a fragrance
clusters of fragile flowers
Naked Ladies
melting morning dew.

Negotiation

A quiet calm descends upon the scene,
the stars are yet to quantify their worth.
The berry bushes cluster, red and green,
your body pressed against the tempered earth,
absorbs vibrations in the fading light.
The lever that controls the force in you,
released by silence, till the dark of night,
crowds in around your existential view.
The bounty of this land fulfilled your dreams,
gave and gave with pastoral rewards,
and streams of vigour flowed, refilling streams
of yearnings you construed in simple words:
    interpreting, your vista laced with time,
    reticulates the banks you cannot climb.

Boarding School in the Fifties

Grouped and fenced and gated at the school –
we found our way with caution, soon immersed
in sport and competition, where one rule
bewildered us: the last shall be the first.*

The Sisters in their habits dip and glide –
kindly women, robed with warm intent.
Concessions and exemptions were denied.
We lived the rules and learned what austere meant.

Freedom lost, lights out! but hidden deep –
a future, shining bright far, far away.
A book beneath the blankets, helped us keep
our dreams, that morphed as scope with each new day.

The rights we had as dreamers, to explore
another world, with literature our guide.
We thrived and grew, the simple truths we wore,
bore faint resemblance to the truths outside.

Now aged, reflection makes the memories feel
that friendships lined our days with fields of green;
how rich, how unexpected the appeal:
now first, now last, now everything between.

* Matthew 20:16

Southern Ocean Live Show

Tasmania

Silver dolphins
surf the rolling bow waves –
swift in air, slick in ocean play.

We face the rocky cliffs,
rugged in the churning swell.
A new, more brittle act is underway:

> breathing rocks erupt –
> fur seals in wild abandon
> haul their slippery mass onto a ledge,
> wallowing in the ice-cold spray.

Tourists grip the deck rails,
exclamations, raincoats, hoodies, chill,
all clamour in disarray.

Shearwaters drift with the wind,
flying low, head towards the shore,
swift in air, slick in ocean play.

Gannets dive like darts.
An albatross watches the show,
wheels, turns away.

Where the Poems Hide

Like a shellfish that's stuck to a pier,
or the waters backed up at a weir,
    silent they wait,
    for release at the gate,
how I hope that they don't disappear.

Then the waterfall rushes with glee,
the oysters are rife in the sea.
    I'm suddenly pleased,
    the pearls that I seized,
are the poems that just came to me.

My arms are all fringed with chenille
that mimics the joy that I feel.
    They sway in the breeze,
    as light as you please,
and my tail feathers shimmy a reel.

Seeds of Summer

The flax crop is caging air,
trembling flowers tender blue,
whimsical sensations,
    rows we wander through.

Barley grain is forming,
ripened husks appear,
stem to head, with fullness,
    threshing time is near.

Whiskered oats in clusters,
bending in the winds;
gold the seeds of summer,
    harvesting begins.

Crackle of the stubble,
fingers sieve the wheat,
jute bags sewn and loaded,
    harried in the heat.

Coffee Time

We speak of spring
and blackbirds
carrying feathers,
nesting
in the ornamental grape vine.
I'm distracted.
My mind is on
a discarded banana,
half-mooned on bitumen,
on the white line,
near the school bus stop.

Lake Tekapo

New Zealand

Tea on the grass,
    sun on the hills
        and a bird.
Tiredness, traumatised,
    wind to contend with
        and rain.
Night falls at Tekapo,
    bodies to mend
        during sleep.
Dawn by the lake,
    snow on the hills,
        we rise.
Free as a breeze,
    healed by the night:
        downhill today
            if
                you
                    please.

Queenstown Camping

New Zealand

Surging falls on rocks cascade,
dewy tree ferns, fronds displayed,
lupins yellow, mauve and pink,
snow the sunshine's earthly drink.

Paragliding from the hill,
on the bridge the bungee thrill.
Rivers flowing, glacial blue,
clear and crisp and crystal hue.

Rainbow coloured hot balloons,
campfire stars and welcome moons.
End the day in silent taps;
catch the coloured windblown flaps.

Puddle-talk

Frogs' eggs
spawned in spring.
Curious child
crouched
muddy shoes
oozing footprints
at water's edge,
circumnavigating
with one gentle finger
the jelly shoreline
of foaming amoeba,
reluctant to dent
the centre of froth
in the slimy
bubbling cauldron
of new life.

The Mulberry Tree

For generations past, our roots
replenished by the rich dark fruits,

we staked a claim, sweet juice to drink,
then pegged our claim in purple ink.

Deep down, a force, a mounting swell
of rancour coarse, familial.

No breeze to twitch the crinkled leaves,
until a death a burden weaves.

The tree uprooted where it stood,
our scars like ageing, peeling wood.

A Case of Google-itis

'Hey Biddy! I can't work today
I've been bitten by a bat.'
Well! I've heard some good excuses,
but none as wild as that!

The bat was sick, he'd picked it up,
there was traffic everywhere.
He searched for refuge for the bat,
which flew into his hair.

He swiped and swore and groped around,
in the tangle he was bitten.
He fumbled, fumed and yelled in fear,
with panic he was smitten.

The doctor said, *You might be right!*
and Googled for a cure.
He said, *This is too much for me.*
With bat bites – I'm not sure.

A specialist was well prepared –
an expert – she should know.
She'd dealt with several in the past,
and warned *This could be slow.*

She set him up on special drips,
and needles she thought best;
she tested blood, then calmly said,
Go home and take some rest.

Take some rest? With two weeks wait,
Bat Virus on his mind,
the victim Googled bat bites,
to see what *he* could find.

'An allergy to water!'
'An allergy to air!'
Two things that sustain a man!
The symptoms, listed there.

'Hey Biddy!   I can work today.
Do you mind if I come back?
There's two weeks wait on test results.
My disposition's black!'

'You can't come in with bat-bites
when your job is cooking food!
Don't come near this workplace;
get some pills to boost your mood.'

He's anxious while he's waiting
for results to filter through.
His face is feeling tingly
and the water's stinging too.

The doctor phones, *The tests are clear.*
All good to go! she said:
he's surrendered to the Google search,
and can't get out of bed.

Woomera – Refugees' Day Out At the Animal Park

Sulphur crest preened to a single strand,
he flipped his head to the side;
held flat as a rounded penny,
one black eye, staring, wide.

Quizzical he acknowledged me,
cracked seed with a foraging beak.
The cockatoo greeting, I said 'Hello!'
and waited for him to speak.

He turned to the back of the sterile cage,
ignoring the wild birds' cries,
saw loneliness strut through the quivering gums,
and spread through the clear blue skies.

Kick to kick, while guards stood watch;
the dark-haired boys at play.
Green grass soft in this desert town;
they're released from dust for a day.

ABBA! he said, and *Dancing Queen!*
he turned to his friend by his side.
Together, they laughed in their native tongue,
and in our language, we cried.

Why in a cage? Like us! he said,
with the same dulled look in his eyes.
Futility filtered through shimmering gums,
flung clouds to our beautiful skies.

Palm Beach

Beach-walking
in wet sand.
Waves roll in,
slap the ankles.
Horizon clear –
I could walk off the edge of the earth.

Retracing steps,
looking down,
credible,
heel on toe,
toe on heel –
finding the way back is never easy.

St Paul's Cathedral

No photography please

She watches
he attaches a selfie stick to the front pew
they pose
        backs to the Sanctuary
                heads together
three red flashes glow with cataract magnification.

They disengage
turn to each other and smile
                step forward
        press display
lean in
pay homage to the merit of the photograph.

The light shines yellow through the stained-glass window
above the crucified body of Christ;
the pillars   up
        rising   and
                up
to shape the solid arch
below the rounded timber panels of the ceiling.

The large window
the stern eagle's dark energy
wings open
        ready to soar
                glassed motionless
shielding a pledge beneath the outspread wings.

Compelling, the illicit selfie,
a simple manoeuvre
inferring curiosity
    searching for truth
sanctioning a world
where religion grows restless.

Rhythm of the Night

I saw a child who danced the moon alight
arms outstretched in moving shadows deep
with rhapsody she danced   secure in the rhythm of the night.

The miners and the monuments the stars that shimmer bright
she spread her arms to feel   to gather in   to sweep
I saw a child who danced the moon alight.

The enigma glows   the dancer slows   in time the two ignite
the desert winds rush in   embers of her soul to reap.
With rhapsody she danced   secure in the rhythm of the night.

Her mood, her feet, her face portray an act of pure delight
the outback claypan firm and warm receives her joyful leap.
I saw a child who danced the moon alight.

Hunting creatures hesitate   confounded by the sight
she pauses   closing eyelids   miming images of sleep
with rhapsody she danced secure in the rhythm of the night.

The impact builds, riddle solved, delivers then takes flight
a vision so intense that it may not be mine to keep.
I saw a child who danced the moon alight.
With rhapsody she danced secure in the rhythm of the night.

The Promise

Tribute to Les Murray

Taller When Prone by Les Murray:
A volume of poems – each title a poem –
at the end 'Winding Up at the Bootmaker's';
turned to find fourteen pristine pages,

peered into the blank shadows of the binding,
felt the creamy nap of the paper.
Seeking a lead – an inkling – a thrust of rustic divinity,
read and unread my expectations,

flicked back to the poems to read 'Cattle-Hoof Hardpan',
heard the breath in four short lines,
curiously related to 'The Man in the White Bay Hotel',
coveted the idea of being *unrescued* at life's end,

harmonised a score to the beckoning beat of
'Jimmy Sharman' and the 'Malley Show drums'.
A 'Wyandotte Hen' fluffed up her golden lace feathers
poised on one leg, stared one-eyed through the words.

In the corrugated iron light of the Show Pavilion saw
'Marble cakes in ribboned pens'
tricoloured layers dipping and rising
with the clicking heat and aroma of a wood-burning stove.

I closed *Taller When Prone* on my lap,
untended the memories and moved on.
The sequel would be found in *Waiting for the Past*
with the promise of winding up *On Bunyah* to fill the void.

Italics indicate titles of books and poems by Les Murray.

Layers of a Storm

The International Year of Indigenous Languages 2019

thunder in the *dhalanans* – rumble roar and wane
lightning bolt's vibration flashing gold theatrics
listen as the heat volt trips the thunder's power strip
spins the rustic rooster upon the weather vane

lightning bolt's vibration flashing gold theatrics
streaming from the aether a silver shower of rain
spins the rustic rooster upon the weather vane
toys with the four winds circles with the *dhalanans*

streaming from the aether a silver shower of rain
lightning fork igniting punctuates the earth
toys with the four winds circles with the *dhalanans*
coloured arc descending hovers on the plain

lightning fork igniting punctuates the earth
thunder clap applauding nature's consecration
coloured arc descending hovers on the plain
mulana of the rainbow reflection of the rain

thunder clap applauding nature's consecration
receptor at the storm's core rarefies the air
mulana of the rainbow – reflection of the rain
thunder in the *dhalanans* – rumble roar and wane.

dhalanans – thick cloud
mulana – spirit (Yorta Yorta)

The Cusp of Love

Criss-crossing the world,
over desert, land and sea,
the map of his endeavour
colour-coded by the years,
his footfall struck the flints of love,
climbed the rock of fears,
his passion, dedication
and ambition craft a synergy…
faith hope and charity and the greatest of these is charity*

Blood is spilled in anger
humanity is strained
bruised by brutal energy
clustered flames of fear,
religions boast divinity –
scream too loud to hear;
the epithetic fervour
holds the cusp of love enchained.

* St Paul's Letter to the Corinthians 13:13

Within the Light

If you ask me about the pleasures of my childhood,
I would say the splash of colour
on the top wire of the fence
and black and red feathers
set against a white morning frost,
when the first flame robin arrived in winter,
answers one question.

If you want to know about a quiet place on the farm,
I can tell you that sinking into a partly filled wool bale
at the shearing shed,
with the smell of shorn wool and earth silence,
a skylight and a copy of *Lady Chatterley's Lover*,
is as special a place to read a banned book,
as any I have found since.

If you ask me about trouble
I would tell you about the brilliant blue strychnine bottle,
which by chance the five of us handled.
The stalwart, our eldest brother,
put the tip of his tongue to the bottle
to see what death tasted like.
The hint of poison left him frothing at the mouth until tea.

If you want to know about colours on the farm
I say the eastern rosellas,
lifting, as we checked their concave nest
in an aged, grey, splintered fence post
and hovering against a blue sky,
paddocks green under newborn lambs;
an indelible splash of light that repeats every year.

Goats You Said

Mount Zion – where a shepherd
guards the giddy goats,
as they spring up, flip to the side,
twisting gymnasts, landing lightly.

> Silly Tatong goats on car bonnets,
> eating garments off the clothes line.
> Rampant destroyers, defiant stare,
> playful, deft at material devastation.

Imported house goats,
arriving with the First Fleet.
Substitute for lamb and cow,
zany animals, valued pets.

> Feral goats, eating blackberry and briar;
> natural pests, munching prickly plants.
> Balancing, scaling rocks and ridges,
> talented overactive exterminators.

Proud Billy Goat teams, pulling carts,
horned, Sunday people-movers.
Faithful playmates to rural children –
billycarts on hills, calamitous spills.

> *Lotions candy soaps milk*
> *ghee cheese yoghurt kefir*
> *buttermilk angora-mohair*
> *kid gloves bath milk dips*
> *hide meat cashmere horn*
> *pashmina – hide they should!*

Liberty

He was the tick
    I was the tock
then it came to me
    at the witching hour
that I could be the clock.

Observation

Murray River Hideaway

Heroes of the river,
future stainless-steel boilermakers.
Scientists, mythologists,
white coats and perspex shields
could be your armour.

Night runners of the Murray River;
ringtail possums, this close.
Bare feet, torn in tag –
You're it!

Marshmallows toasted,
forked twigs, red-tipped,
circumnavigate the future,
the man in you, that grows in you,
shining through
in the campfire glow.

You have searched
way back with the ancients,
to find your guiding star.
No stars tonight.
Warmth that goes with autumn rain,
but when they do shine here,
they sparkle through to the heart of you.

This Time of Life

This day when day's weird entrance makes no sound,
our dreams now spent, distinct and snugly framed;
the dialogue is deep, the thoughts profound,
our complex road of exit, yet unnamed –
we fight to keep our place in the parade.
Luminous, propelled, the thoughts we store,
though deeply felt portray a bland façade,
that waves the flags of age, an ageist war.
Look far along the corridors of hope,
look far, right past the memories, to stream
what's woke, what's hype, then up your *Periscope**
and cast around to contemplate the meme:
    the worldwide web can sometimes seem inept;
    the search, the wonder – that's where magic's kept.

* *Periscope* – live video streaming app

Cyclical Changes

Trolls have stalked the Minister for Injections.
Clowns are stripping naked on the greens.
Friends are made; we tally their affections.
Children, seeing short from watching screens.

The world has been entranced by the elections.
Heads of State and subjects, talking Trump,
aware there may be truths and wild deceptions,
the walls he builds too high for folks to jump.

The spider crabs are gathered, having hurried
to moult their shells in shallows in the bay.
They're safe to humans, why should we be worried?
They're two months early, so the scientists say.

The Senate's busy fixing feuds and flaws,
a shopping trend emerging globally,
leaves amateur importers free of laws:
distributors declare the shipping free.

Dancing Brolgas

Brolgas fly low,
almost touching the surface of the lake,
before landing
ankle   deep

to

feed.

Choreographing existence on the verge,
gunugudhulas – the brolgas
dance their ballet,
splaying feathers,
beak to beak
spreading wings
plié and *jeté:*
high stepping spindle legs,
on pointe
these trumpeting brooding redneck swamp birds

    n   g
   e   n
     s   i
    T

in the shallows.

gunugudhula – brolga (Yorta Yorta)

Colours of a Winter's Night

The first hint casts a red glow over stark grey branches,
and the orchard is hooded with the glow,
the reflection painting my windows deep orange,
fading to grey then softly disappearing into night.

A street light shimmers in cold air,
blends with the shadows, so that there is no beginning,
and no end, to where the light is cast
as it quivers a shape with each movement of the trees.

The evening star, sparkling in the sky, beckons me.
A single yellow light that shines the way for other stars;
sprinkled in the cloudy, white splash of the Milky Way;
the evening star, that can be whoever you want it to be.

My mother comes that winter's night, covers me over,
gently tucks me in; stands beside my bed in silence.
The comfort, the linen bib of her bright blue apron,
her knowing smile, blending winter colours with a dream.

Bush Meditation

Steeped in rich narration, Earth Mother watches;
floating single feather, falling softly down.
Corroboree in Dreamtime, hallowed sense of place.

Dance moves *jukurpa*, fire pit burning,
lean bodies gleaming, flicker in the flames.
Steeped in rich narration, Earth Mother watches,

pulsing with the rhythm, brooding with the dance,
flowing through the stories ancient tribal grace.
Corroboree in Dreamtime, hallowed sense of place.

Spirit in *yidaki*, lingering, droning;
breath relates the music, courses in the veins.
Steeped in rich narration, Earth Mother watches.

Posture in *dadirri,* language seeping through,
deep in meditation, solace in the passion,
Corroboree in Dreamtime, hallowed sense of place.

Visual, lamenting, vested in the rituals,
smoke plumes hovering, feather's intervention.
Steeped in rich narration, Earth Mother watches,
Corroboree in Dreamtime, hallowed sense of place.

jukurpa – dreaming
yidaki – didgeridoo
dadirri – meditation

Expression – At Site Sixteen

Converge on the Goulburn

Come dress me in my coloured clothes
and twist and wind my listless curls,
to style my airs as beautiful,
and thread me, so my beauty swirls

in patterns round the passing crowd.
The hurdles, with the rustic stands
and perfumed autumn in the air,
we weave and mould with joyful hands.

The ropes and silken shredded scarves,
tell stories that we live, like yours.
The ancient music fills the air,
a welcome through our city's doors.

A social act, as kneeling down,
the guests engage with quiet intent.
A boy, his head inside the frame,
by chance he weaves a wonderment.

The intonation in our world,
the loosely woven, structured words,
inclusive as the moulding hands
of children, shaping precious birds

and nests and eggs, as children do.
The parents roll and shape their art –
lotus flowers, cast in clay.
Here, *Splinter Artists* play their part.

The sum of all who worked today,
threaded beauty through our veins.
Spun us new, with coloured threads,
in and out and knotted skeins

of wool. The patterns, random, formed
and twisted in the final play,
for stories come from many lands,
performed and shared with us today.

'When does the weaving find an end?
How do you know the end is near?'
*'There is no end, the endings meet
and converge in the atmosphere.'*

As evening comes, the breeze still warm,
a moment where the baskets sway –
untouched, their sinuous skirts reveal
the dance of what's achieved today.

The flowing waters here converge,
words are written, yet unread.
The words weave, as the rivers run,
marry clay and silken thread.

'Banksia' Poetry Group – 2019

Shepparton Villages

The Muse sews aeons past in seams of truth.
The sea birds call – above the waves they soar,
and poets writing love, envision youth
still listening for the hoofbeats on the moor.

The search begins, the paper daubed with age,
the lustre of a shell, the rolling dunes.
A lantern lit at dusk, lights up each page,
till daybreak drapes her curtain on the moon.

A key inserted in an oaken drawer,
a long and flowing gown, a silken coat.
The raiment swept aside, to step ashore
at sunrise, from an ancient poling boat:

>   the images, bereft of likes and looks,
>   engage us face to face; we're sharing books.

Migration

On the top branch
of a native pine tree
a flame robin landed.
Harbinger of winter,
he puffed his brilliant red breast
to show: *I'm back!*
cast a wary glance,
then chose to preen.
The plain grey female
grooved her flirty dance moves
on our winter green.

Winter in the Washhouse

Grey, coarse concrete troughs beside the copper.
Firebox crackles red. Kindling flames pop

in rhythm with the ridges. Thud, push, splash,
on the glass washboard, up-down, rub and scrub.

Copper stick handy, wood worn white and smooth,
she chose the clothes for washing, one by one.

Unfolding for inspection to the light,
stains scrubbed; items tossed in troughs –

contrasts, hot and cold were well in hand;
steaming sheets hung heavy on the stick.

She worked each garment through the final rinse,
wringing, draped them knotted on her arm.

Seasons met her head on, as she worked,
sodden clothes, the basket at the door –

she hauled each heavy load along the path.
Crisp the frosts, paddocks dripping green,

she sought each ray of sun, each hint of breeze.
Feel that! her hands, so cold against my cheek.

A single strand of wire, pegged in style,
colour-coded schemes, the socks in pairs,

long timber props, pushed high, secured the line,
shirts and dresses billowed in the wind.

The rainy days and still days were a test.
The timber horse was given right of way.

Adjusting, moving, open fire burning,
she stroked the clothes and stoked the dying flames.

Acknowledged here, her energy and care,
we glowed in shirts kept white with bags of blue.

The softness in our clothes, the washhouse vibe,
wafts down the decades, permeates the page.

Alaphilippe

Tour de France – 2019

A strategy, a glance might foil your case;
your purpose you adhere to on the course.
The ruins and the splendour of this place,
emblazoned on each pedal spin; the force

in stage wins, sprints, the hard-won fight for glory.
It's known that every book starts with one word;
here stage by stage, and page by page, the story
relived by teams, in dreams that history spurred.

The push, the pull, the climb, the finished stage;
the yellow jersey glows, the lonely cold,
the alps, the winding gradients – you engage
a smaller gear – it's here *le Tour* is told:

> each man, his quest, without the pall of pride,
> takes hope and flair and anguish on the ride.

Kaleidoscope

A rich mosaic forms the colours
of new thoughts, purple and gold.
Not of temples or churches,
objects or ornaments –
just the inward beauty of a thought,
surging towards a distant goal –

>breathing
>>with the colours
>
>watching
>>patterns change
>
>fragments
>>click and fall
>
>a shifting
>>live display
>
>of myriad
>>form and frame
>
>like a poem.

Newell Highway – 2019

paddocks parched
crops fail...
interstate convoy

                                  b-double swerves...
                                  echidna pauses
                                  crosses the rumble strip

roadside spill
pitchforks   trailers...
news spreads

                                  orange dust cloud
                                  a mob of sheep...
                                  for sale

felled timber
crawling creatures scramble...
bleeding carcass

                                  cactus limp and faded...
                                  flattened veins open to receive
                                  intravenous rain

Drought

He
taps the tank
knuckles tightened
against the dull thud of the first rung
and the next and the next
galvanised
echo the emptiness.
Wisdom
leans a moment
against the grey-dry timber of the tank stand
lingers that moment in the eye of the storm.
Scans the sky
tastes the pink dust
feels the pink dust smother the breath
colour the clouds
pink-dry in the dull wind
Turns
follows the thin thread of his recollection
along the gravel path
through the orchard
leans his thoughts
in one hand
on the weathered stump of the stile.
Walks
wide of the beehives
to the sheep yard
feels the first drops of rain
smells the wet fleece
stands unsheltered.

Art in the Singing Garden

Toolangi – Victoria

There are dapples in the forest drawing outlines on the bark;
the Listener of the Poetry is wandering quietly through.
It was here he learned the lyrics of the magpie and the lark.

He was the 'Poet Laureate' of the Push, the Stoush, the Nark;
expression in his Song Book, recomposed *Ter tell yeh true!*[1]
There are dapples in the forest drawing outlines on the bark.

The soil is soft beneath his feet, all still and quiet, but hark!
Singing morning has begun,[2] birds are hopping two by two.
It was here he learned the lyrics of the magpie and the lark.

He harvested the birds' song, forest-scrounger, to embark
on briefings, till the springtime's court upheld his verse anew.
There are dapples in the forest drawing outlines on the bark.

The Singing Garden, ageless, fielding colours light and dark,
the twitter in the bushes then a *flash of gold and blue.*[3]
It was here he learned the lyrics of the magpie and the lark.

Scholar of *What Bird is That?* he fanned the Muse's spark;
flame burned rich with story, *time is fleeting, worms are few.*[4]
There are dapples in the forest drawing outlines on the bark.
It was here he learned the lyrics of the magpie and the lark.

1. *The Songs of a Sentimental Bloke*, C.J. Dennis, The Intro.
2. *The Singing Garden,* C.J. Dennis
3. 'Morning Glory', C.J. Dennis
4. 'The Blue Kingfisher', C.J. Dennis
'The Ground Thrush'.
What Bird is That? A guide to the birds of Australia, by Neville W. Caley.

Big Dam

Somewhere,
between the warning time
of the fictional waterdogs
and a fear of brown water,
was a short span of youth,
where a deep, dark, dam
       held no fear for us
          and we slid in,
            sinking
              knee deep
                into silt,
                swam
                  naked
                    at midnight.

Death of a Star – Hen 2-437

If I study the moon in a curious yet soft way,
I see a tear on rounded cheek,
as she watches the dying star swell into a giant red ball,
in one last defiant burst of life,
shedding layer upon layer of self –
to interstellar dust.

If I close my eyes, then open them softly,
still searching the Milky Way,
I fancy through a mist, the angel wings
of the planetary nebula,
outstretched – symmetrical;
a quivering, sacred presence in the cosmos.

If I gaze at the stars, wide-eyed, enchanted,
they seem to shimmer whiter
in farewell and salutation,
my imagination flickers
then a star-seed finds foundation
and the planetary lineage manoeuvres a solution.

Hailstorm

The sky was black.
A bird
wings shot with green
flew low over my car.
Suspended by the wind's force
framed in my windscreen
flying above the bonnet
getting nowhere
pounded by the rain,
until a sudden updraft
took it away.

I parked the car in the shed
as hailstones fell,
hoping bird
that you made shelter too.

Wax Print Fabric Bag – Design No. 13455

To know what is in our hearts
first you must learn our songs
know the land and our family   our way
the land   the family   the songs   we stay together
African women   the fabric   our sacred rock
we live and love to the beat of the drums

we dance to the beat of the talking drums
drums that beat to the beat of our hearts
worries and fears sing in the night   near the rock
stories we tell   dancing away fear   deep in the songs
we read the past in ancient carvings   afraid together
that what we read could somehow tell our way

no one speaks who can tell us   who can know the way
we learn the language of the Lunna   the Dondo   the drums
they speak to us in their language   boom-boom   together
in a key like no other   a motif   and it opens our hearts
we had long heard the message hidden in the songs
audible in the drumbeat   echoing around the rock

we must go   leave quietly now   past the ancient rock
in darkness   along the known river   away from family
hearts throbbing with the memory of our songs
far away from the sound of the talking drums
through the forest   no beat to beat with our hearts
afraid now   into the unknown   we move together

quickly first then slowly finding strength we stay together
sorrow bleeds and blocks us   we think of home   our rock
sound and safe the African shrine   etched in our hearts
we long to touch the tender flesh, hear the cries of family
we feel courage pounding in us   strong   like the drums
we repeat a mantra   over and over   words from our songs…

It is time to learn the music   the meter   the rhythm   songs
of our new land   we are safe   growing in strength together.
we speak of Africa   our people   remember the talking drums
on dark days we are brittle   our hearts are hard like rock
our shrine will guard our land   we want to tell our family
we are safe   they must wait   they are with us in our hearts

Envoi

The music of *yidaki*   the Lunna   the Dondo beating together
the talking drums   songs   Uluru   two rocks melding a shape
in our hearts   our family there   with us in our dreaming.

Lunna and Dondo – African talking drums
yidaki – didgeridoo

When the Bubble Bursts

The probing impulse punctures the allure
of words that breathe, the breath within resounds;
a theme that seemed so blindingly obscure,
emerges, new and robust, and rebounds.
A strident force that panders to the truth,
removes the doubt and subjugates the fears,
to link the spring with misty dreams of youth.
The mind in conquest, seizes and reveres
some lofty words, that simmer slow and age,
reduced in time, by human sense, or fact,
a back foot, firmly planted on the stage,
to hold and keep the vagrant words intact:
>to stream and shape, to temper or rescind,
>till bubbles spill their colours in the wind.

Pins, Poems and Protocol

With a trolley full of groceries and no cash on hand
proceeded to enter my pin – *seven-one-six-two* –
spare hand hovering ready to pay…

Distant as the echo of a ski lift in a whiteout
the numbers had immobilised
no sequence clue or rhythm to recall
my shrew-like brain had paralysed them all.

I created a new pin   selected four numbers
saturated with clues and meaning.

Used the new foolproof pin for two years with aplomb.
With a trolley full of groceries and no cash on hand
on just another ordinary day   proceeded to pay…

From somewhere in the dark recesses of my brain
the fickle first pin – *seven-one-six-two* – resurfaced
devoid of functionality   flashing at me,

my replacement pin this time annihilated.
Stricken I stared at the floor.
Thought and thought until I knew nothing.

The employee glanced at the queue
avoided my gaze   with wilful ageism
hit the supervisor bell   hard   twice.

Horoscope

In beauty, love, divinity, the Deva's powers bide,
to group within the Galaxy and glimmer in the light,
seeking, free in space, to catch the next terrestrial flight,
and *Major Tom* turns up to be the extraterrestrial guide.

The Star Seed Workers congregate, to rearrange the stars
pack their plans in meteorites that hurtle down to earth,
Major Tom now mindful of his chosen path, and worth,
wonders at the tweet by Trump: *the moon's a part of Mars.*

The Gaia and the Titans, and the Bearers of the Light;
Major Tom delighted, takes them all aboard as crew.
Ancestral Mother demonstrates the *Planet Earth is blue,*
while *Ground Control* directs the Deva's flight.

The planets wander aimlessly, unbridled and adrift,
still Major Tom, his helmet on, believes that he can find
ancient downloads, lineage, predictions unassigned:
but David Bowie's rock and roll has caused a cosmic shift.

A shift that split the horoscope, alas not free from ills,
your future, in the day to day, and dawn to dusk, and noon;
at midnight Major Tom arrests a Star Sign on the moon:
your failsafe future guaranteed, by stealth and *protein pills*.

'Space Oddity' lyrics by David Bowie

Norfolk Island

Cascade Falls
rocky shoreline –
James Cook plaque

                moonlight through pines
                lantern shadows flicker –
                mutineers of the *Bounty*

unhallowed ground
convicts mass grave –
ocean keening

                ruins of a chimney
                rubble-rock carvings –
                piken hihis

colours of the light
ocean floor alive –
Phirestar's friends

                thatched earthen floor
                bower in the bushes –
                a rooster crows

golden-orb-spider
backward weaves a web –
post-to-veranda-post

piken hihis – picking hihi – periwinkle

Full Moon at Winton Wetlands

A shadow slid from the shoulders of the moon,
spread a silver soft greyness over the stilled machinery,
slipped into the cracks and crevices of the dry lake bed,
found the tracks of the red-bellied black snake,
followed the scent to the fox's den,

searched for the hallowed secrets of Lake Mokoan,
in tides of cracked clay and concrete house foundations,
exposed twisted pathways and skeleton gardens.
The ancient voice of the fresh water soak,
echoed the call of the liberated spirits of the swamp.

A yellow glow spread across the land,
followed the shadow's every move,
reflected access along the torn-down channel banks,
lit passages for tortoises, frogs, creatures of the night:
for curlews   calling   calling   calling

Blue Moon 2018

'The moon will be close to the earth – sounds and thoughts
will be amplified, images magnified; magic happens.'
– Dr Lisa Shortridge, meditation leader, Shepparton

Tumbleweed waltzed
the 'Blue Danube'
around my clothesline,
dipping and pausing,
lightly touching the hot gravel,
gratefully inured to lunar magic.

The wind died away;
linked,
the tumbleweed paused,
frivolous
wavering gently
against the fernery wall,
forward and back,
forward and back,
heat driven,
awaiting the wind swirl
that would choreograph
the next dance.

Leaving the City

Walking to the train station
I'm at ease with the world,
dodging other travellers
in the crowded street.

From my window seat
I watch the rhythmic friction –
metal on metal,
silver circles,
spinning wheels
of a passing goods train.

Erroneous the visual echo,
my reflection, our direction,
neither here nor there.

Maypole
Elegy

Memory of your warmth
rises with the lifeforce,
flows as pastel ribbons,
mauve and pink and blue
dipping   rising
dancing   falling
over   under
softly with your breath,
catches our breath;
a rhythm to hold onto
while we wait together
for this last long night to end.

Yearnings fade,
Mother's breath weakens.
She takes a hand
either side of the bed –
arms gently lifting,
weakly falling:
she sings – we all sing
'Auld Lang Syne'.

        Epitaph

        No cymbals clang
        no sound is heard
        in the deep
        and blessed comfort
        of the grave.

Spare

I found, in an edit of *Within the Light*,
one page with one word – spare –
the page, otherwise blank,
needed something concise.

I could mention a blackbird
that flew into the window pane just now,
explain how the poor bird's legs
jut out of its lifeless plumage.

I could check the subject matter
in the poems either side;
insert a mid-range thrust,
working within topical guidelines.

I could write about tightrope walking;
shine a light on the skill, the challenge,
the courage and balance
of the tightrope walker.

I could write about repetition,
which often goes unnoticed in an edit.
I found an excessive number of birds –
and mentions of Paul the Apostle, *Within the Light*.

A raven turned up twice – now thrice!
I lost a poem once. Wrote it, then lost it –
about the Dead Sea, too much salt, how you float,
you can't sink. You can never rewrite lost poems!

I know! The EGO explodes onto the page!
The I word has infiltrated my train of thought again.
What a good idea! Spare can be the title –
poems don't always need to be elegant.

Gratitude

for Peter McGurgan

In late February
a pair of kingfishers
tunnelled a burrow
in the top layer
of a round hay bale.

An unusual nest,
monitored
surreptitiously
by the farmer
at feed-out time.

A breeding-pair
with warm intent,
eggs hatched,
chicks co-parented
then released.

Tunnel entrance
shabby now,
breeding rights renewed;
a new cycle about to begin.
One kingfisher,

halcyon singer
looks below,
dubs the Earthy Farmer,
tweets his awesome majesty
three bales high.

Ode to Quasimodo

1.

He lived to ring a carillon, the bells of Notre Dame.
Deformed at birth, his energy defied his awkward gait.
Hunched, he roamed the city streets, familiar to the crowd;
he knew their fear, felt the scorn, the vestiges of hate.

The rustic bells were so designed to meld their varied tones.
The *ringers* in the transept knew to wait for his command.
He signalled go excitedly, then swinging on the rope,
combined the chimes in spires that pealed across the land.

He named the statues and the bells; they spoke to him of love.
The church, responsive, held the hunchback safely in her womb.
His body strong, his energy and spirit knew no bounds,
and Notre Dame's cathedral, in time became his home.

As Quasimodo's joy was fierce, the bells rang loud and long.
Hearing damaged from the noise, his deafness was profound.
He surrendered to the malady by choosing not to speak:
the only crime – his *differences*. The bells his only sound.

2.

A baying mob had gathered round to validate his crime.
He felt the whip, the lashing; he was flogged until he bled.
Tied with ropes he suffered, with his anguish fuelling pain,
a windlass pulled the wheel, his heart grew cold with dread.

A priest rode in upon a mule; he didn't intervene.
Quasimodo watched him, as he paused, then turned away.
Hope now lost, his differences were shredding with his skin:
Water, he begged weakly; his world began to sway.

One eye closed, helpless now – dazed with grief and pain,
he sought relief in silence, as he wildly shook his head.
Quasimodo cried that day, he shed one single tear,
pleading, desperate – *Water* was the only word he said.

Pierrat[1] had timed the whipping; it was over – he was gone.
The victim fought his bondage, jeers grew wild and loud,
he heard in his delirium, the aftersound of bells,
he thought he saw the gypsy girl[2] emerging from the crowd.

The noisy mob was silent, as the child approached the wheel,
her beauty and her innocence – the contrast was sublime.
He stared in abject hopelessness. He pulled against the ties.
She held the gourd against his lips, denying them his crime.

*

3. Fire at Notre Dame Cathedral, 2019

As flames flared high, the searing heat disturbed an ancient soul,
seen clambering down the outer face beside the burning spire.
Quasimodo climbed the tower and grabbed Emmanuel,[3]
bestrode the bell, gripped his legs, ignored the raging fire.

He watched the frightened crowd below lamenting in the street.
The flames reflected red and yellow ripples on the Seine.
The crowd became his audience and Quasimodo cried,
'Hear this! The bells of Notre Dame may never peal again!'

1 & 2 based on the story 'The Bell-ringer of Notre Dame' by Victor Hugo, *The International Library of Famous Literature*, Volume V

1. Pierrat Torterue – the torturer of the Châtelet.
2. Esmerelda, the gypsy girl.
3. Emmanuel was cast in the 1600s – the large bell survived the fire at Notre Dame Cathedral on 15 April 2019.

Cinquain

boomerang
warm wind blowing,
whoom-a-whoom   throwing,
light touch   easy go   no return
wanya

wanya – boomerang (Yorta Yorta)

Australian Identity

raven
statue-still
standing watching discerning
evoked the eerie *Bust of Pallas*:
crow.

'The Raven', Edgar Allan Poe

Cosmic Dig

fossil
eons-old   quirky
orbiting   clumping   lurking
silently   endlessly   in outer space
Arrokoth

Arrokoth – sky, Powhatan, eastern Virginia

Remember

the kiss
of the maple leaf
as it brushed your cheek
and shed a tear
as you left
and
you
let
the
tear
linger
cold
on your face.

Festival Art

It takes time to rap the senses, tap the essence of a theme,
the elements of Festival portrayed in works of art;
delving in the colours, in the collage, in the dream,

we search, engage the vision – detect a hidden gleam,
then touch the tender daisies on the tendrils, one by one.
It takes time to rap the senses, tap the essence of a theme.

Rebirth, a meditation, an emerging complex scheme
evolving, the design, one wing. The story aches in me;
delving in the colours, in the collage, in the dream.

A striking snake, a totem, etchings abstract and extreme,
detonate the artist's pen, embellish and adorn –
it takes time to rap the senses, tap the essence of a theme.

A man within a woman, shadows trace the quarried seam
of birth, of death, evoked by scale – cohesion of the pair,
delving in the colours, in the collage, in the dream.

Profile facing profile, one embossed – the two extremes
tie art to evolution with a flower child's tendrilled hair.
It takes time to rap the senses, tap the essence of a theme,
delving in the colours, in the collage, in the dream.

'Call to Create' to Goulburn Valley Writers' Group, Shepparton Festival 2020. Ekphrasis poem inspired by winning festival artworks by local artists.

Mysterious Bird

The Muse has played some tricks on me at times,
today I said, quite firmly,
Never More!*
The words belong to Poe
and little did I know
my mind would still be plying me with rhymes.

I want to read now –
read *Forever More*;*
my poesy has finished, I am shut!
My creative mind has closed,
I won't be versed or prosed:
my song is sung, the lyrics and the score.

* 'The Raven' by Edgar Allan Poe

Breakdown

The pallid light of dawn peels back the mind,
and sunlight streams a readiness for thought,
too harsh the golden beams that truth outlined,
the earth ignites the harrowed path you walked.

By day you navigate through fields of stress,
that billow in the brain and take control,
and scatter there, revealing vividness;
when colours burst, the garish memories roll.

Evening draws the alchemy of peace,
and shadows hold their place in the dim night,
they give a shrouded view where visions cease,
with silence muting beams of faded light:

>   from sun to moon diurnal petals fall;
>   your mind in chaos relegates them all.

#Beachwalk@80

'Gather ye rosebuds while ye may' – Robert Herrick

It's morning and the tide is in retreat;
the sand flats ripple patterns, as an art.

Soldier crabs are working to a plan,
safety holes and tunnels to complete.

Searching in the rockpools as we play,
our musings yield an atmosphere of joy;

thoughts recoil, discerning, growing restless:
we snap the latch on what we thought to say.

Rock to sand to pool, our day's complete,
when whistling ducks swing in on grassy dunes.

Osprey swoops; reclaiming occupation.
A turkey, now outnumbered, in defeat,

hides in the vines and scrub that line the beach.
Gulls that dip, and dive, and scan the waves,

land lightly on the sand to check the scene,
stand, sentry on one leg, just out of reach.

We laugh and splash, in sodden sands we play.
The soldier crabs have scarified the land

and from old age, we hasten a retreat;
utilise each comeback – while we may.

Armstrong Beach, Queensland

Storm

Listen
as the lightning burst
trips the thunder's power strip
spins the rustic rooster
upon the weather vane
striking in transmission
Spirit of the Plain.

Watch
as the lightning fork
punctuates the earth's floor
flashing gold theatrics
crush the storm's vein
Streaming from the aether
a silver shower of rain.

Wait
to hear the thunder roll
clapping in the cloud form
applauding with vibration
rumble roar and wane
lowered arc of rainbow
consecrates the rain.

from 'Layers of a Storm'

A Chance Meeting

A single maple leaf
falls
in winter.

Azalea blooms;
stamen beads
on slender styles
quiver
in the melting morning.

Tinges of a deeper pink
stream from the throat
spilling a warmth
mirrored in dew.

Captured leaf stem
plunges
into funnel depths
in a futile union;
star-leaf
lifeless
rests against petals
vibrant and fresh.

Coupled in winter sun,
an ornamental blueprint
for procreation.

Union of the Arts

Cautious,
moving in the artist's wake,
breathing,
in the deep,
uncharted sea
of meditation;
sensing,
seeking shape
in brushstrokes
that might glow
and speak to me.
Stirring,
moving through the phase
that holds
the gist,
the sheen,
the artist's working hand;
the pen
in random strokes across the page
becomes a brush
that paints a single strand;
a rim,
the golden framework of a plan:

collage and phrase
both interwoven there,
connect
evolve and merge
to shine a light
on dreams
that every artist needs to share.

Written for Rachel Doller's painting *Evolve*,
the theme of Shepparton Festival 2020.

Pressed Flower

A small dried flower, thin and frail,
had bled her nectar on the page,
smudged the Gospel of St Paul,
scribbled pansy, dried with age.
My sister Mary placed it there,
saved it in the Scripture's bower:
tentative I touched with care
the small dried flower.

No Through Road

The Old Bridges of Howlong

The sound of the adze, the pointed timber posts;
  posts now worn have stood the test, unfazed.
Unfazed through drought and fire and raging flood;
  flood that washed, and fire that leaped and grazed;
grazed and licked the red gum timber piles.

  Piles stand strong and straight, I gaze around,
around the gum trees and the native scrub.

  Scrub that lines the river, on this ground –
this ground – the camp, the horses' scent long gone.

  Gone. The magpies warble, and their song –
their song brings back the past. I touch the rust,

  the rust-encrusted ancient bolts, so strong.
Strong. They grip the bridge planks they engage;
  engage the river's stories, told through time.
Time has choked the access now; on the river flows.

  Flows where shapes and shadows never age.

The five bridges of Howlong were built around 1907
and were replaced in 2001.

Windsong

With a dingo howl
heat sweeps over the ridge,
ruffling feathery tufts,
brandishing the cadence of the wind.

Heat sweeps over the ridge,
foraging earth's floor, harvesting desolation,
brandishing the cadence of the wind,
fissured slopes designing a drought.

Foraging earth's floor, harvesting desolation,
wallaby mother stares, lifting front paws,
fissured slopes designing a drought,
while winds petition the living – and the dead.

A wallaby mother stares, lifting her front paws,
ruffling feathery tufts,
while winds petition the living – and the dead,
with a dingo howl.

Buddhist Sound Bath

The mallet raised, the pause, the surge has come;
the golden notes twang softly on the gong,
a single stroke, well primed, resounding dong.
A pause, a passive moment, then the thrum
that emanates exquisite from the drum.
Thoughts, concerns and foibles roll along,
tuned in with peace, the copper plates, the song.
When mind detects the visual in the hum,
and flippant thoughts deny the poignant view,
the tonal hosts caress the gongs more lightly
to overmine the noise the silence spurns.
Percussion, twirling crystals ringing through:
    haunting tam-tam rhythms tremor slightly;
    inside the vibe a scented candle burns.

The Colour of Love

Discussion with Samuel, aged 8

'Did your mother see the world in black and white?
　were shadows greyed by darkened sun,
　was colour unseen by everyone,
　was moonlight dulled by soulless dark of night?

　Were thoughts and dreams in black and white,
　did warmth feel pink, though skies were grey,
　did darkness lead the ghosts away,
　could candle glow light up a sombre sight?

　In happiness which colour could she feel,
　how could she know the beauty and the glow
　of rainbows, sunsets, flowers as they grow.
　If they were black and white, could happiness be real?'

'If we look closely, Samuel, and let our thoughts run free,
　though black and white the photos you review,
　we see her world was coloured by the happiness she knew;
　her aura, in our memory, encircles you and me.'

When Summer Burns

Shepparton – January 2020

A garden boy stands amongst the agapanthus
petal-ball flowers laced purple and white.
Silvereyes scatter leaf litter.
In ten years sun has bleached the statue pure white.

The boy faces the sunrise, awakens the breeze
a playful breeze that tickles the wind chimes.
Hydrangea leaves wilt. Gardenia buds open overnight,
scented, curled petals velvet-white.

Noon, the wind jostles the chimes,
tosses the clapper against the bamboo tubing,
blends an eerie sound at the window. Wind and chimes
whine in chorus; various – dark and white.

A smoke haze clears. Dust storms smother border districts.
Forest fires burn along the coast.
Intermittent windpuffs blow random layered shapes
into passive flocking clouds, powder-white.

A north wind blows up, shakes the trees, loosens tendrils
on the vines. Cconjures up a sense of dread with *ABC News*
Warnings. Coastal residents flee, embers ride the wind,
smoke, an ominous messenger, billows white.

Firefighters deployed, waging the next war
against the juggernaut, the raging, new fire front.
Two familiar magpies sing, carolling their loftier view,
uniform feathers contrast, black and white.

Self-isolation

Covid-19

I saw a dullness on every page
and every word *Within the Light*
became dull,
then
I saw the shadow
creep upwards
from the bottom right-hand corner
spreading doubt,
like a cloud
that cowered over the title,
glowered over the page,
a foreign, frightening thing,
and I knew it was right
to set the poems aside,
allow the words to wait,
away from the dark
anxious world;
away from me.

The Poet's Climate Prophecy

Drifts in mists and breaths of breeze
and rain and snow and bursts of golden light.
The temperature is rising,
glaciers shrink, the forest's trees ignite.

Through winter's chill, winds wail and moan,
mountains, valleys solid under snow.
The springtime melt renews the streams,
cleansing waste and debris with the flow.

The planet's fickle climate,
conniving and cajoling till it's spent.
Expending warmth in sunshine,
becalms our fears – then plots a flood event.

Wands of drought waive amnesty,
explicit in extremes to launch the heat.
The sun steals vital nutrients,
parches land to cultivate defeat.

In supercharging cloud-forms,
the lightning sparks explode in stricken veins.
Thunder claps roar cloud to cloud,
as shock waves bump across the arid plains.

Then raining – raining – raining,
the strumming throbs in puddles on the ground.
Fused coloured strands of rainbow,
a blaze of promise in the rhythmic sound.

We modify our carelessness,
scientists give notice, based on fact.
The change, earth's degradation,
urgently imploring us to act.

Ill winds blow in – easterlies,
they coil in feisty gusts; we feel the call.
We watch the trees – they're whispering;
the windmill turns, disordered by it all.

One simple yet momentous task;
revisit ways we've lost! The poet said,
when *earth is made to smile again*,
she'll guarantee *all living things are fed.**

---

* from 'Song of Rain' in *Selected Verse of C.J.Dennis*, 1950

A Moment in Time

Layers peeling, white suede petals tucked and folded,
firm with promise.
Engaged by the allure,
she reached to pick the late magnolia bud,
summer heat long gone,
some trees leafless in the winter cold.

Curious fingers, premature in their quest,
began to expose the hard core;
outer petals, lifted one by one,
dropped down on the kitchen bench.
Casing released,
a perfect flower bloomed, cupped the errant stamens.

Unclosed, the perfume spread,
red tips of filament, blood of the birth.
She cradled the moist flower on her palm,
breathing new, scented air;
coiling petals, collected on the bench,
already bruised with rust.

Supermarket Dilemma

Lockdown, July 2020

Diminished by loss of social language,
missing connection in meetings with strangers;
real, unspoken kindnesses in eyebeams.

Heads down, we enter the fray, craving space,
clearing passage, cribbing at the markers,
diminished by loss of social language.

Calculating strategic moves, we pause,
feigning glazed propriety, plundering
real, unspoken kindnesses in eyebeams.

This viral hopscotch: invisible tor:
jump-to game: alone: find the cross: turn:
diminished by loss of social language.

Subservient civilians, square by square,
seek the flow in chaos, the throb of life;
real, unspoken kindnesses in eyebeams.

Time soon to plant the seeds of tomorrow:
cultivate a new, new life – not reigned in,
diminished by loss of social language;
real unspoken kindnesses in eyebeams.

The Final Edit

The notes
lit up like fireflies
lifting in the updraft
frilled white
at the edges,
mischievous
winking
words
drifting
down
pastel grey
at our feet:
slivers of ash
obliterating fear.

Acknowledgements

Acknowledgement is gratefully made to the editors of the following publications, in which some of these poems have appeared previously. Some have been edited.

Goulburn Valley Writers' Group
tamba, *Songbirds* anthology, editor Pat Patt, 2018

Ginninderra Press
Strings of Life, 2011
'Woomera, Refugees' Day Out at the Animal Park', *First Refuge*, editor Ann Nadge, 2016
'Rhythm of the Night', *Wild*, editor Joan Fenney, 2018
'Cyclical Changes', *I Protest!*, editor Stephen Matthews, 2020

Quadrant
'Speaking of Language', 'Negotiation', 'St Paul's Cathedral', 'The Promise', 'Appraisal', 'Art in the Singing Garden', 'When the Bubble Bursts' '#Beachwalk@80', 'Storm', 'The Final Edit'

Splinter Contemporary Artists
'Expression at Site Sixteen' was commissioned and written in direct response to community art activities developed and delivered by Splinter Contemporary Artists, Shepparton Festival, Converge on the Goulburn, 2019

C.J. Dennis Society
'Art in the Singing Garden', *100 years of Jim of the Hills*, editor Daan Spijer; First Prize in the Toolangi C.J. Dennis Society Poetry Competition, Open Section, 2019

www.ingramcontent.com/pod-product-compliance
Lightning Source LLC
Chambersburg PA
CBHW070925080526
44589CB00013B/1435